KIDNAPPING: MEANING AND ORIGIN: POLITICAL AND OTHER CAUSES

SCHOLAR

Contents

CHAPTER I

Introduction

In criminal law, **kidnapping** is the unlawful confinement of a person against their will, often including transportation/asportation. The asportation and abduction element is typically but not necessarily conducted by means of force or fear: the perpetrator may use a weapon to force the victim into a vehicle, but it is still kidnapping if the victim is enticed to enter the vehicle willingly (e.g. in the belief that it is a taxicab).

Kidnapping may be done to demand for ransom in exchange for releasing the victim, or for other illegal purposes. Kidnapping can be accompanied by bodily injury which elevates the crime to aggravated kidnapping.

Kidnapping of a child is known as child abduction, which is a separate legal category.

Kidnapping of children is usually done by one parent or others. The kidnapping of adults is often for ransom or to force someone to withdraw money from an ATM, but may also be for sexual assault. Children have also been kidnapped for the commission of sexual assault.

In the past, and presently in some parts of the world (such as southern Sudan), kidnapping is a common means used to obtain slaves and money through ransom. In less recent times, kidnapping in the form of shanghaiing (or "pressganging") men were used to supply merchant ships in the 19th century with sailors, whom the law considered unfree labour.

Criminal gangs are estimated to make up to $500 million a year in ransom payments from kidnapping.

Kidnapping has been identified as one source by which terrorist organizations have been known to obtain funding. The Perri, Lichtenwald and MacKenzie article identified "tiger" kidnapping as a specific method used by either the Real Irish Republican Army or Continuity Irish Republican Army, in which a kidnapped family member is used to force someone to steal from their employer.

- Bride kidnapping is a term often applied loosely, to include any bride "abducted" against the will of her parents, even if she is willing to marry the "abductor". It still is traditional amongst certain nomadic peoples of Central Asia. It has seen a resurgence in Kyrgyzstan since the fall of the Soviet Union and the subsequent erosion of women's rights.
- Express kidnapping is a method of abduction used in some countries, mainly from Latin America, where a small ransom, that a company or family can easily pay, is demanded.
- Tiger kidnapping is taking a hostage to make a loved one or associate of the victim do something (e.g. a child is taken hostage to force the shopkeeper to open the safe). The term originates from the usually long preceding observation, like a tiger does on the prowl.

Kidnapping has sometimes been used by the family and friends of a member of an alleged cult as a method to remove the member from the alleged cult and begin a deprogramming process. Deprogramming and exit counseling have been used with the purpose of getting alleged cult members to abandon their groups' beliefs. The danger presented by cult groups has been used by deprogrammers to justify using the extreme act of kidnapping to get alleged members to change their allegiance away from the group.

CHAPTER II

Meaning and Origin

The original meaning of *kidnap*, dating from the late seventeenth century, was "steal children to provide servants to the American colonies," from *kid*, "child," and *nap*, "snatch away." After the particularly notorious Lindberg baby kidnapping in 1932, the U.S. Congress passed a law allowing the FBI to investigate all kidnappings. Today the word *kidnap* includes all abductions, of both children and adults.

The verb ***kidnap*** originally meant **to steal or carry off children or others in order to provide servants or labourers for the American plantations.**

During the last four decades of the twentieth century, the most notorious and widespread abductions of children in Africa have been closely associated with armed conflict in such countries as Angola, Burundi, the Democratic Republic of Congo (formerly Zaire), Mozambique, Rwanda, Somalia, Sudan, Sierra Leone, and Uganda, among others. On the other hand, pervasive poverty, large demands for child labor, and the huge profits to be made by child-marketers have created a massive trade in African children within and outside of Africa. Some of the children sold in this network are abducted. Less visible but more persistent and equally deleterious, child abductions thrive in the context of a host of socio-cultural practices.

In pre-colonial Africa, large-scale abductions of children occurred in the course of the trans-Atlantic slave trade in the fifteenth through nineteenth centuries in West Africa, and in the eastern and central African Arab-Swahili slave trade, which peaked in the nineteenth century. In both cases, children were sold into slavery to lands beyond the continent. Traders created intricate conduits for conveying abducted populations from the interior to the coastal trading houses. Perpetrators included individual traders, brokers, royal houses, and European partners, the latter stationed at the coast.

Additionally, localized ethnic conflicts produced limited and intermittent abductions of children as war hostages during the pre-colonial period. The common practice was to integrate the children into the families and social structures of their captors. The children were looked upon as additional social capital vital for productive and reproductive activities.

As illustrated in the case of Zena (discussed below), the practice of abducting child brides has evolved beyond customary sanction and has increasingly attracted greater attention in judicial circles. There is also an emerging phenomenon of infant abductions traced to desperate childless women. Children of unsuspecting mothers in hospitals and crowded townships become easy targets of such desperate women. It appears also that there is a market for abducted children among childless women who feign motherhood upon returning to their homes. A breakdown of extended family networks has robbed childless women of the benefit of access to communal child-rearing responsibilities. This may have forced the women to child abduction.

Elsewhere, amidst political instability and the emergence of religious cults, there are reports of child abductions associated with ritual sacrifice. Whether the children are targeted for their innocence, and hence ritual purity, for their vulnerability, or as vital social capital, adults, in their efforts to transact political, economic, or social-religious contracts, brutalize children.

CHAPTER III

Kidnapping in the 21st Century

At the beginning of the twenty-first century, civil wars constitute the single major cause of child abduction in Africa. The scale, complexity, and brutality of modern, armed conflict-related child abductions dwarf the precolonial situation by far. Both rebel forces and governments perpetrate the abductions. Abducted children serve as domestics, porters, messengers, and general camp followers. Girls, some as young as ten, become sex slaves for the soldiers. Boys, and some girls, are forced to perform armed combat duties.

While internal precolonial abductions sought to integrate their victims into the captors' society, modern abductions seek to isolate, separate, brutalize, and intimidate the children into malleable errand boys and girls. Thus, in addition to being forced into regular combat, abducted children are also forced to commit rape, torture, and killings, sometimes directed at fellow children. This serves as initiation into a life of violence, and serves as warning of what will befall them should they become recalcitrant, or try to run away. In order to elicit and sustain such criminal responses from the children, some captors are reported to drug the children. Thus children become both perpetrators and victims of violence.

Present-day concentration of settlement has made children more vulnerable to abductions. Schools are popular hunting grounds for rebel armies. For example, between 1994 and 1998, the rebel Lord's Resistance Army (LRA) in northern Uganda abducted about 8,000 children, most of them school children. In April 2001, the UN High Commission for Human Rights reported that more than one-third of the more than 26,000 abduction cases recorded so far in Uganda were children under the age of eighteen. Some were as young as nine. In 2002, most schools in northern Uganda had been shut down for fear of further abductions. In Angola, child soldiers were as young as eight.

The LRA is also said to sell children in exchange for arms and ammunitions. The resurgence of slavery, and the juxtaposition of child abduction and the trade in weaponry, constitute new variables in the child abduction syndrome. The cordial relations between the LRA and the Sudanese government imply government complicity in the trade in children.

Modern Africa has surpassed other regions in using children to fight its wars. This is a new development. Abducted children comprise an appreciable proportion of child soldiers. In some countries, including Sierra Leone, Angola, and the Democratic Republic of Congo (DRC), child soldiers have played pivotal roles in civil wars. For example, in the DRC, it has been claimed that child soldiers, referred to as *kadogo,* or little ones, constituted the majority of the rebel soldiers used to oust dictator Mobutu Sesse Seko in 1996.

Straddling an international military network, these child soldiers operated among Ugandan and Rwandese soldiers. The new regime in the Democratic Republic of Congo continues to use demobilized child soldiers on street patrols, while in rebel-held sections of the republic continuous child abductions have forced parents to pull their children out of schools. In Angola in 1994, 12 percent of the rebel Unita forces were children.

The astronomical resurgence of a clandestine trade in children in West Africa is an open secret. Some of these children are abducted. The trade is especially rampant in Benin, Burkina Faso, Cameroon, Côte d'Ivoire, Nigeria, Gabon, Central Africa Republic, Mali, and Togo, countries that are not engaged in civil wars. This is a marked contrast to the era of the trans-Atlantic slave trade, which fuelled wars that in turn provided war captives.

The current trade in children constitutes a wide network of porous, cross-border trade conduits including destinations in Europe, the Gulf states, and Lebanon. Demand for child labor in the domestic, sex, and drug trafficking networks, coupled with massive profits from these circuits, has revived, and massively expanded, child-kidnapping practices.

The majority of the children thus traded are girls, up to 95 percent in the Benin-Nigeria circuit. They are between the ages of seven and seventeen. Storage depots, office markets, and ships for transportation have been established to facilitate the disbursement of kidnapped and other enslaved children. In a 2002 debacle in Côte d'Ivoire, children abducted from Mali for employment in the cocoa sector were set free by the Ivorian government, but not before an international uproar. The government of Côte d'Ivoire was quick to blame immigrant Malian cocoa producers and residents from Burkina Faso for the abductions.

In the precolonial period, the general practice of forced marriage also involved the abduction of girls below the marriageable age, with or without the knowledge of their parents. In some regions, this practice had the social sanction of the community. In others, the practice was represented as jestful theatrics, implying that there was no forced removal and that the screaming bride was merely joking. While still evident, today the practice has been criminalized and in some cases the abducted child brides, or their parents if they are not party to the abduction, at least in theory have re-course to law. In fact, however, their legal position is ambiguous. This is demonstrated by an ongoing legal battle in Swaziland, which is complicated by the fact that the prospective bridegroom is a man of great social and political standing. In October 2002, eighteen-year-old Zena Mahlangu was abducted from school by two royal messengers to await marriage to thirty-four-year-old King Mswati III. The king is reported to have nine other wives. Zena is a victim of a convoluted practice still sanctioned by customary law but criminal under common law.

While historically the Swazi royal household was expected to consult with the families of prospective brides, this did not happen in Zena's case. More daunting is the fact that under Swazi law neither the king nor the queen can be arrested, sued, or prosecuted. Efforts to make the king a defendant seem unlikely to be successful. In a dramatic turn of events, press releases in late October 2002 stated that Zena Mahlangu had declared that she was ready to be married to the king and that she had settled into her new life. This change will likely bring the litigation to an end.

Modern child bride abduction is often occasioned by males' desire to marry a virgin in the belief that virgins are free from HIV/AIDS. The loss of their virginity upon marriage ensures that even if they flee from their unwanted marriages most of these girls would not return to their homes since this would bring dishonor to their families, and on their ethnic group as a whole. The juxtaposition of a modern scourge and an age-old practice render girl children even more vulnerable than before. So too do child and maternal deaths due to the undeveloped physiology of child mothers. Child marriages also increase school dropout rates among the girls, depriving them of economic independence in the long run.

To the victims, abduction is psychologically traumatic. The torture, killing, and exploitation of abducted children increasingly call into question the conscience and morality of a whole continent. The conniving of a cross-section of global participants, driven by struggles for political power, and by avarice, sexual depravity, and individual inadequacy, have created a horrifying milieu for a large number of African children. All abducted children are robbed of their childhood and most are blatantly exposed to an adult world of senseless killing.

CHAPTER IV

Political Causes of Kidnapping

Political kidnapping is kidnapping which is conducted to obtain political concessions from security forces or governments.

Political kidnapping has been happening for more than a millennia. Occasionally, political kidnapping has vast impacts, such as the kidnapping of Chiang Kai-Shek creating the Second United Front and uniting China against Japan at the start of World War 2.

There were series of kidnapping of senior diplomats during the 1960s and 1970s. By the end of the 1960s, political kidnappings were evidently profitable.

For a long period, political kidnapping was usually a Latin American phenomenon, with some few overlooked incidents in Europe. After the 1990s, when the interest of tourists and businessmen increased in Asian and Pacific countries, the kidnappings also became a means to support the political motives of newly established dissidents groups, such as Abu Sayyaf's group, which has conducted numerous political kidnappings.

Arab history features a concept known as 'desert diplomacy'. Per the Gulf Research Center, "The objective of this traditional activity was to apply pressure on hostile tribesmen by issuing demands, the fulfillment of which would lead to the safe return of their son or daughter. Demands would be, as they are today, financial, moral or political; although hostages would rarely be killed. Nevertheless, retention of the hostage for some years was not unusual. The kidnappings taking place in Iraq today are ones far departed from the traditional practices of Arab (and indeed, other nations) tribal warfare which were governed by a strict protocol, ensuring decent, gentle and safe treatment of the captives."

Various groups in the Palestinian Resistance and in the Lebanese Civil War (1975-1990) employed political kidnapping as a method.

Al-Qaeda began using political kidnappings around 2004.

Political kidnapping happened in Latin America before the 1970s, but it was then that the number of kidnappings accelerated.

According to the New York Times, "So far this year [August 1970], there have been at least 18 successful or attempted kidnappings in Latin America. Among Latin Americans, the victims have included a former President of Argentina, the Foreign Minister of Guatemala and the former Foreign Minister of Colombia. Among foreigners, the victims have included ambassadors, consuls, labor, commercial and military attaches and even consultants with no governmental positions." Kidnappings were used as a tactic by urban guerrilla fighters. Stated goals included release of political prisoners, for ransom, embarrassment of officials, and straining ties between countries.

Often, though not exclusively, kidnappers attack while targets are travelling in cars. A car or truck carrying terrorist forces will force the target's car off the road, proceeding to hold them at gunpoint until they surrender. Frequently, cars used are stolen then abandoned, which hampers police investigations.

CHAPTER V

Other Causes of Kidnapping

There are many causes of kidnapping around the globe, including:

- Unemployment
- Poverty
- Illiteracy
- Religion
- Greed
- Politics
- Corruption

Below, we'll examine each cause individually.

Unemployment

The high unemployment rate in many countries has forced citizens to find other ways to make money—and some of those ways are illegal. Kidnapping a rich person can be a lucrative business. A cash-strapped unemployed person may believe that when he kidnaps someone who is rich, he may be able to become rich himself.

Poverty

Any person who lives below $ 1.25 a day is living below the poverty line. Poverty can propel people toward crime as a way to make ends meet. Sometimes, a person who is poor might believe that kidnapping or other illegal acts could provide the necessary money to start a new life—a life that will no longer involve crime.

Illiteracy

Illiteracy is the inability to read or write. When people know how to read and write, they can gain the skills they need in order to become educated, get a job, and live a productive life. Literacy and education can also be an important foundation upon which to build a deeper understanding of moral judgment and decision-making.

The kidnappings and bombings perpetrated by Boko Haram, the militant Islamic group in Nigeria, are caused by illiteracy, at least in part. The leaders of this group feed their men false information, which the men cannot disprove by reading outside sources. Boko Haram fighters engage in suicide bombings, killings, and kidnappings. They are told that if they die while carrying out their mission, they will inherit the kingdom.

Religion

Many kidnappings in the world today have their root cause in religion. Some people love their religion so much that even when it teaches them something that is wrong, they believe it is right. One religious leader may want to take over another group—and order his men to kidnap his rivals.

Greed

Some people are not contented with what they have and wish they could buy more and more things—whether it's fancy clothes, cars, houses, or jewelry. This kind of person may turn to crime to make more money. A wicked businessman can kidnap his business rival for a large ransom to become richer.

Politics

Corrupt politicians may arrange for the kidnapping of their opponents. Sometimes, they do this so that their opponents will make concessions or change their votes on the issues.

Corruption

A society where corruption is rife is likely to experience a high level of kidnapping. The truth is that if a government is corrupt and embezzling public funds, citizens may react by kidnapping those corrupt politicians in an attempt to recoup some of the stolen money.

Kidnapping Often Involves Torture or Rape

Kidnappers sometimes choose to torture their victims so that they can force money out of their relatives or associates. Sometimes, they may even torture for fun. One form of torture is rape.

CHAPTER VI

Effects of Kidnapping

For the victims, there are many negative consequences of kidnapping, including:

- Psychological trauma
- Fear and lack of trust

Psychological Trauma

The negative psychological effects of being abducted are huge, especially for a child. Depression, anxiety, and post-traumatic stress syndrome (PTSD) may last a lifetime.

Fear and Lack of Trust

In a society where the incidence of kidnapping is high, fear limits people's lives and actions. They will always move with caution as they do not know who might be the next target. The rich surround themselves with security guards because of their fear of getting kidnapped.

CHAPTER VII

Global Problem and Worldwide Issue of Kidnapping

A Global Problem

Kidnapping is a global problem that affects countries all over the world—from the United States and Mexico to many countries in Africa, Asia, and beyond. Governments are working hard to address this problem and ensure that the perpetrators are captured and brought to justice.

Kidnapping refers to the abduction and captivity of a person, typically to obtain a ransom. Sometimes kidnappers hold their captives longer in order to demand more money from the victim's relatives or associates. It is a wicked act.

No matter the level of difficulty anyone is facing, that is not enough reason to choose kidnapping as an option to survive. There are many causes of kidnapping, including unemployment, poverty, religion, political issues, and so on. The practice can be reduced with governmental involvement.

A Worldwide Issue

The rates of kidnapping in Europe, North America, and South America are attracting worldwide attention. The practice of kidnapping has become quite lucrative for some, and there are criminal groups that have made it their business model.

In Mexico, with its history of drug-related violence and police corruption, kidnapping is an old story. According to the U.S. Department of State, Mexico suffered an estimated 105,682 kidnappings in 2012, and in 2013 the number reached 131,946, the highest number on record.

The disappearance of children in the United States is not unheard of, either, and it is a problem that police and other agencies are working hard to address. According to the National Centre for Missing and Exploited Children, roughly 800,000 children are reported missing each year in this country.

CHAPTER VIII

Solutions to Kidnapping

There are solutions that may help reduce the rate of kidnapping, including:

- Training strong anti-kidnapping agents
- Monitoring the activities of the police
- Serious punishment for offenders
- Job creation

Training Anti-Kidnapping Agents

Any country that wants to fight kidnapping successfully must hire and train capable agents to combat the issue. When law enforcement agencies are actively involved, the incidence of this crime can be lessened.

Monitoring the Police

Reports show that the police are involved in some kidnappings. Notable examples have occurred in Mexico. Eliminating the criminals within the ranks of law enforcement is key.

Seriously Punishments for Offenders

Mild punishment does nothing to deter criminals. When the government treats kidnappers harshly, fewer abductions will occur.

Job Creation

Generating jobs for citizens, especially for the youth, can have a huge impact on the fight against crime. When people are gainfully employed, they do not need to commit crimes.

A Work in Progress

Kidnapping has caused disorder in societies today. Kidnapping is a global problem with many root causes, including unemployment, poverty, religion, and politics. Each of these root causes must be evaluated and addressed in order to eliminate this terrible scourge once and for all.

9 798887 830360

Printed by Libri Plureos GmbH in Hamburg, Germany